for Christopher Blake at the age of six

The Snowman

Easy piano picture book

Original story and pictures by Raymond Briggs
Music and words by Howard Blake
Illustrations by Dianne Jackson

ff

Faber & Faber
in association with Highbridge Music and Faber Music Ltd

This book first published in 1986 by Faber & Faber Ltd
in association with Highbridge Music and Faber Music Ltd
3 Queen Square, London WC1N 3AU
Music drawn by Allan Hill
Printed in England by The Thetford Press

The Snowman is recorded on CBS 71116 Cassette 40-71116

The following sheet music of The Snowman is also available

The Snowman complete (full score; piano score)
The Snowman (suites for flute and piano; violin and piano;
Bb clarinet/tenor saxophone and piano)
Walking in the Air (piano/vocal; easy piano; guitar; recorder and piano;
flute and piano; Bb clarinet/tenor saxophone and piano;
trumpet/cornet and piano)

British Library Cataloguing in Publication Data

Blake, Howard
    The snowman: easy piano picture book.
    I. Title   II. Jackson, Dianne
    823. 914[J]   PZ7

    ISBN 0-571-10076-7
    ISBN 0-571-10074-0 Pbk

Also available:

Swan Lake:
Easy piano picture book

ISBN 0-571-10078-3 (paper) 0-571-10077-5 (cased)

Hansel and Gretel:
Easy piano picture book

ISBN 0-571-10083-X (paper) 0-574-10082-1 (cased)

The Nutcracker:
Easy piano picture book

ISBN 0-571-10080-5 (paper)

The Snowman

HOWARD BLAKE

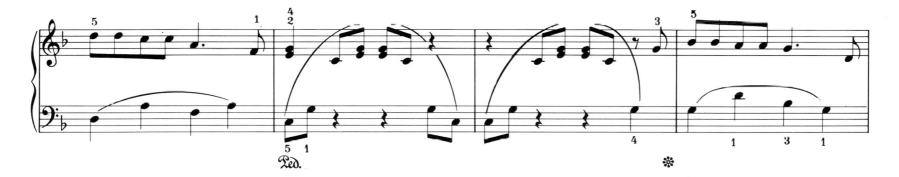

It was a cold, cold winter's night. In a cottage in the country, tucked away beneath the hills, a little boy lay sleeping. Snow began to fall, lightly at first, and then with giant flakes, which started to settle on the ground.

At first light of morning, the boy turned over, yawned, and sat up. He ran to the window and looked out. Everything was covered in snow . . . the garden, the fields and the distant hills.

He got dressed as fast as he could. When he was ready he hurried down the stairs. At the back door he put on his boots, his scarf and his woolly hat and walked out into the snow. And it was at exactly this moment that he got the idea of building the snowman.

Building the Snowman

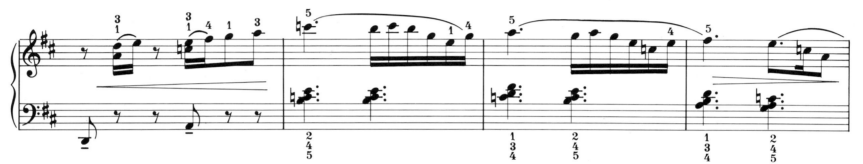

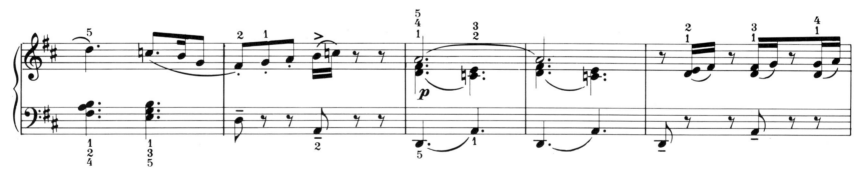

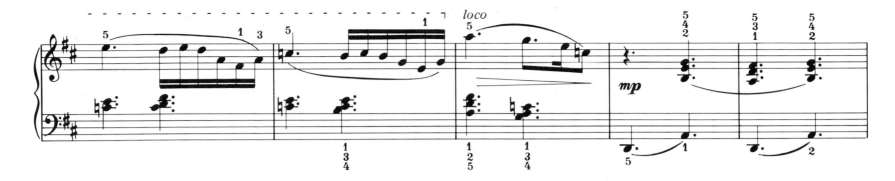

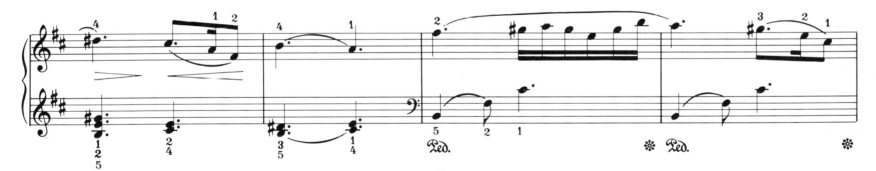

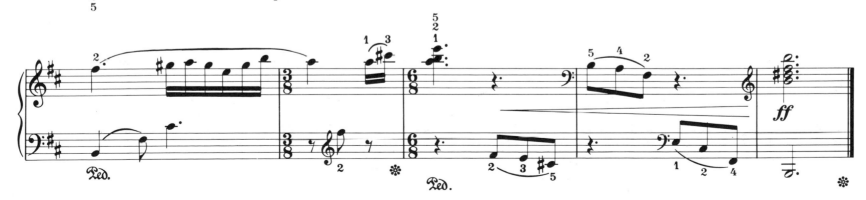

He built a great column of snow the size of a man . . .
and a great big snowball to go on top of it. Then he
fetched a scarf and a hat, a tangerine for the nose,
and coal for the eyes.

At last the snowman was finished, and the boy stepped
back and looked at him. He seemed to be smiling.

By this time it was getting dark and the little boy had to go indoors, leaving the snowman standing all alone, out in the middle of the garden.

It was time to go to bed. Soon the boy was fast asleep. In the middle of the night he woke . . . got up and tiptoed down the stairs, feeling rather cold. He looked out at the snowman through the glass panels of the front door. Suddenly, while the boy was looking at him, the snowman . . . *moved!* Then he actually started to walk towards the boy . . . and they shook hands. 'Come in?' said the boy. 'I'd love to', said the snowman. Together they tiptoed into the living room. The snowman thought it was wonderful.

9

The snowman sat himself down in a comfortable armchair. Then
with a start the boy realised that the snowman was sitting too near the
fire. He realised that he might melt if he got too hot, so he pulled him
out of the chair and hurried him out of the room to the kitchen,
which was cold and dark. He leaned down and opened the fridge
and a waft of cold air came out. The snowman loved it. For him it was
just like sunbathing.

'Let's go upstairs', said the boy. In the boy's playroom was a music box. They wound it up and danced to it.

Music-Box Dance

Tempo di valse

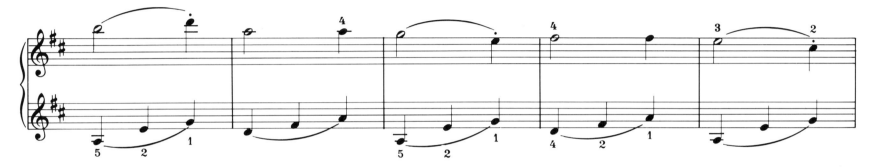

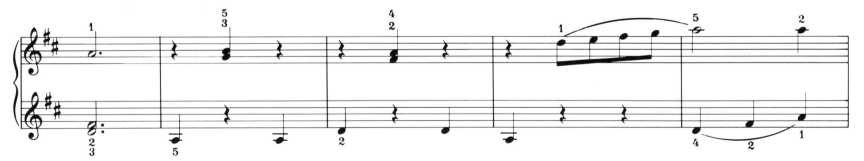

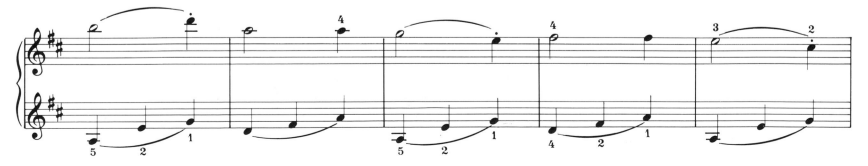

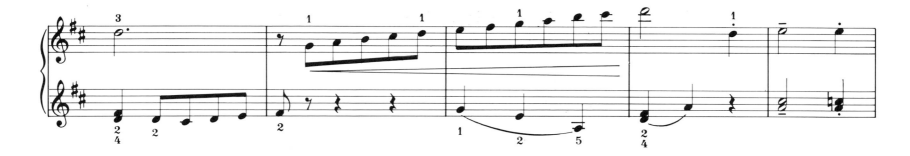

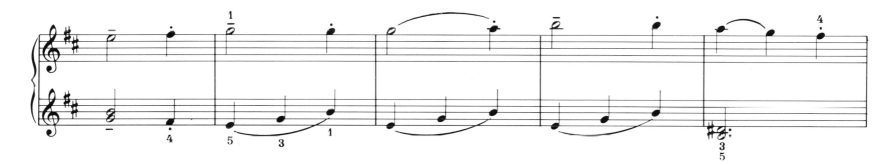

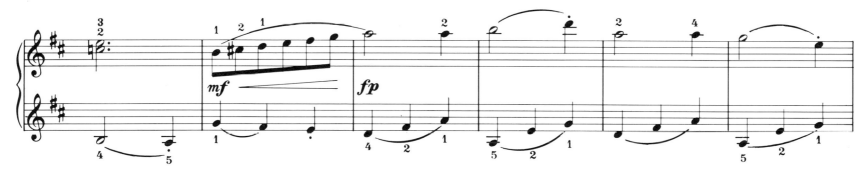

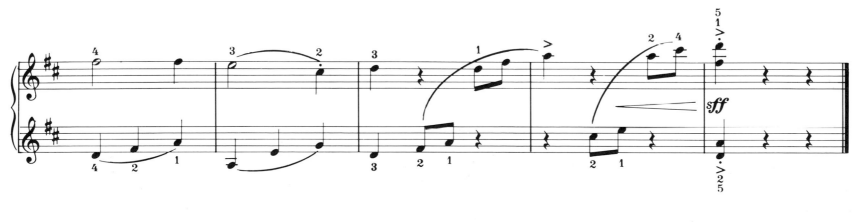

At the end of the dance they both collapsed on to the floor, with balloons and teddy bears all around them.
'I've got another idea now', said the boy. 'Come with me and look out of the window'. Outside they could see a strange dark object. Nodding to each other, they tiptoed silently down the stairs, out through the front door and into the open air. The dark object seemed much bigger now they were close to it, and whatever it was was covered up with a big black tarpaulin. Summoning all his strength, the boy went up and pulled it off. Standing there was a bright, shiny new motor bike.

The boy pointed out the controls to the
snowman, turned the key in the ignition,
turned on the headlight, and suddenly the
snowman was on the bike and racing round
the garden. For a second he stopped; the little
boy jumped on behind him, and then . . . they
were off!

Motor-Bike Galop

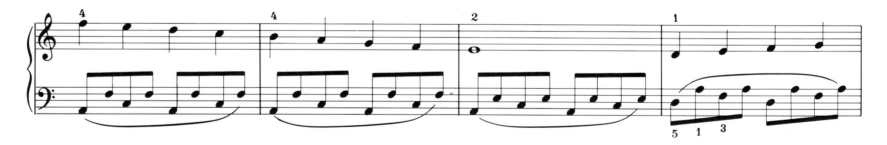

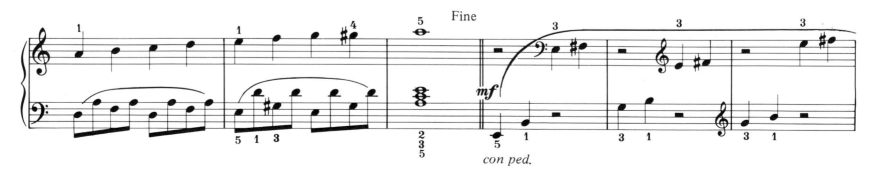

They came back to the garden. Without warning the snowman
gripped the boy firmly by the hand and began to run . . . out across
the garden, faster and faster, bounding and jumping, until suddenly
the boy realised that they were . . . flying! . . .

Walking in the Air

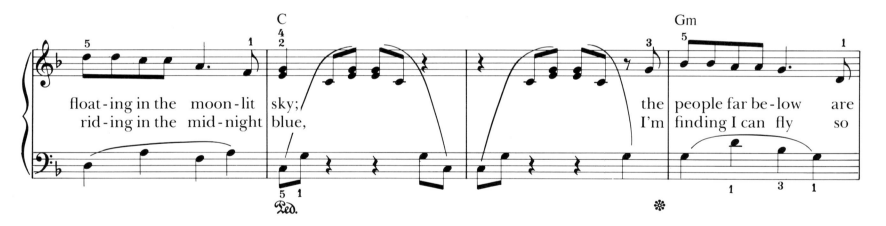

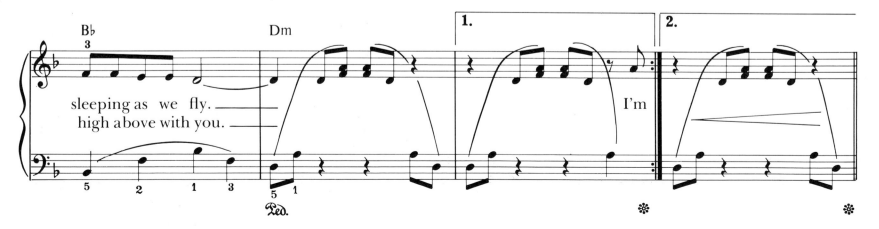

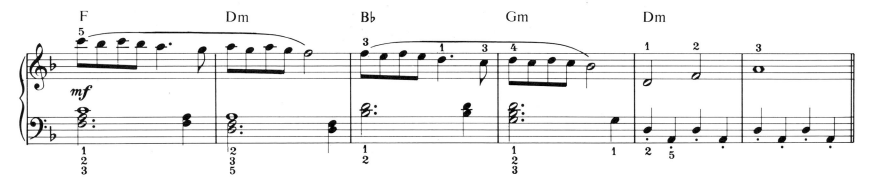

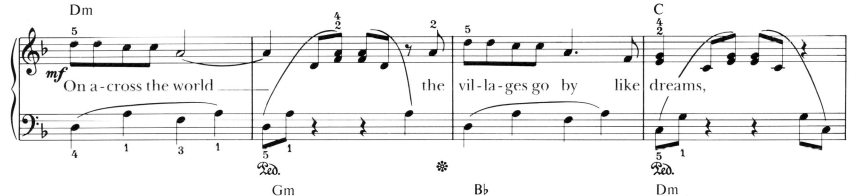

On a-cross the world _____ the vil-la-ges go by like dreams,

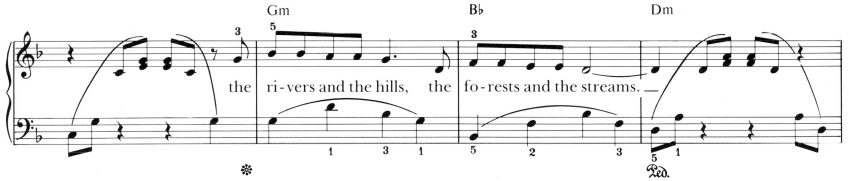

the ri-vers and the hills, the fo-rests and the streams. _____

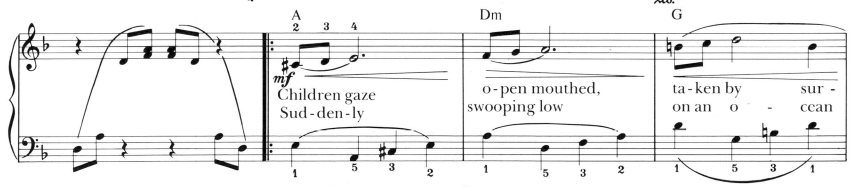

Children gaze   o-pen mouthed,   ta-ken by   sur -
Sud-den-ly   swooping low   on an o - cean

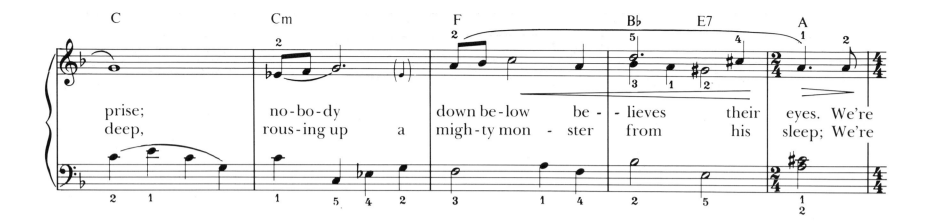

prise;
deep,

no-bo-dy
rous-ing up   a

down be-low   be - lieves
migh-ty mon - ster   from

their
his

eyes. We're
sleep; We're

surf-ing in the air, _____
walk-ing in the air, _____

we're   swimming in the fro-zen   sky,
we're   danc-ing in the midnight   sky

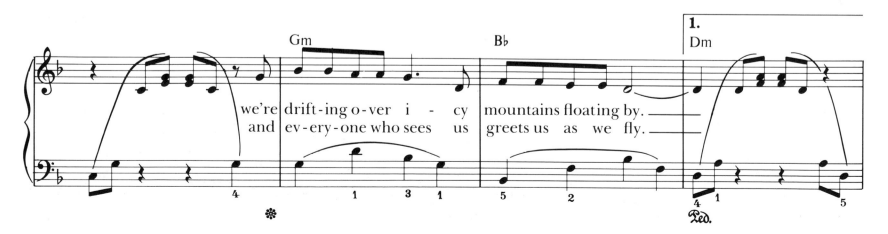

we're   drift-ing o-ver i - cy   mountains floating by. _____
and   ev-ery-one who sees   us   greets us   as   we fly. _____

1.

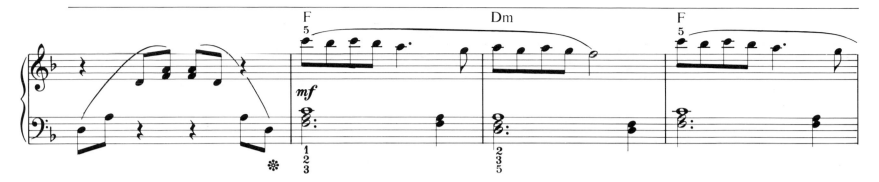

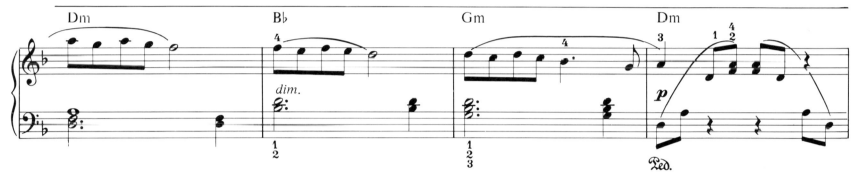

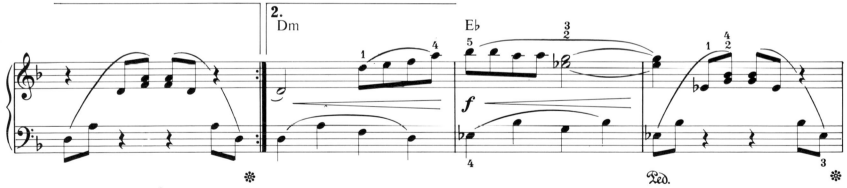

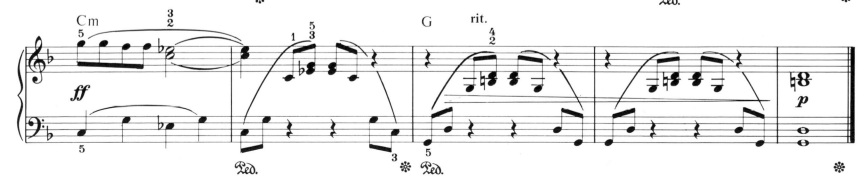

They landed silently in the frozen North. All around them was a great forest of pine trees, laden with snow.

But somewhere ahead they could hear music and see lights. There in a clearing a Christmas party was taking place, and all the people at the party were snowmen – more snowmen than you could ever imagine in your life. And right in the middle of them, radiating good cheer and smiling from ear to ear, was Father Christmas himself. 'You're just in time for the Dance of the Snowmen', he chuckled . . . and clicked his fingers.

Dance of the Snowmen

Allegro giocoso

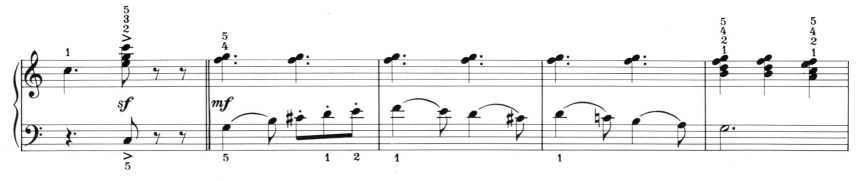

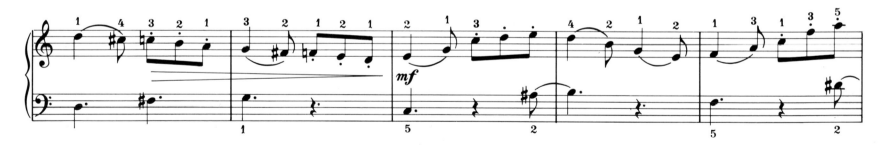

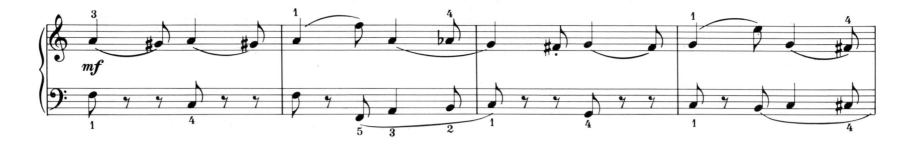

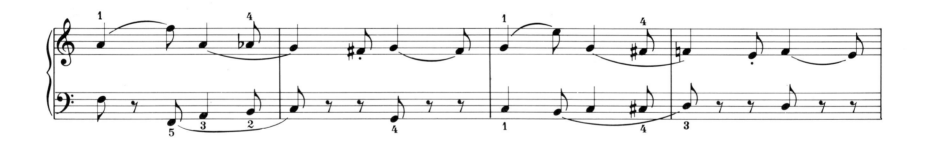

When the party was all over, Father Christmas led the boy and the snowman to a stable. Light spilled through the door, and inside they could see the reindeer which he used to pull his sleigh. Father Christmas gave the boy a lovely blue scarf as a present, and he put it on.

It was time for them to go. The snowman gripped the boy's hand, and once again they started to run . . . faster and faster . . . bounding and jumping until they were flying!

At last they landed in the garden again, and together walked slowly to the house. The little boy shook hands with the snowman and went up to the front door. But the snowman waved, and the boy ran back and gave him a great big hug. Then the boy went indoors, and very soon was fast asleep. Next morning when he woke the room was ablaze with sunlight. He put on his dressing gown, ran downstairs and opened the front door. The sun felt warm on his face. He ran out into the garden and saw . . . a little heap of melted snow, an old hat, a tangerine, a scarf and a few lumps of coal. . . . But the snowman was nowhere to be seen.
For a moment the boy thought that the adventures of the night before had been nothing but a dream. But then he felt in his pocket, and the scarf that Father Christmas had given him . . . was still . . . *there*.

Moderato

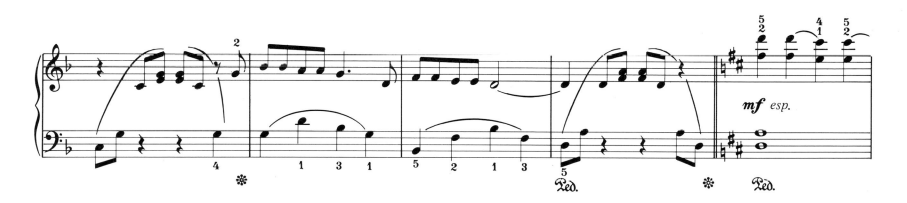

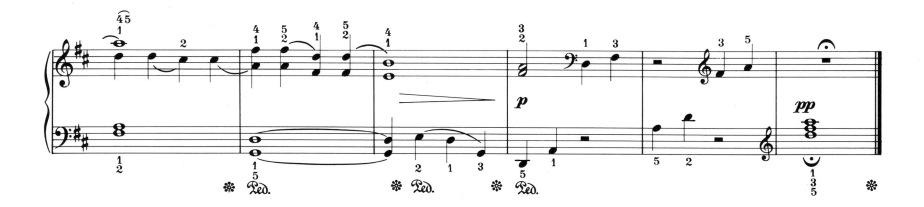